At the beginning of all time God made
our world.

At first it was dark and empty. But
God knew his power would change it
into a beautiful place.

God made light, so there was
darkness and light.

'That's good,' said God.

3

There was water everywhere.
God decided to keep some water in
the clouds and some on the earth.

So God made the sky for the clouds.
He kept some of the water stored in
them for when he needed rain.
'That's good,' said God.

God moved the water into special places on the earth and called them seas.

The water looked beautiful. The light shone on it. The edges of the water curled over onto the land in white waves.

In some places it roared around rocks and threw sparkling spray up into the air.

'That's good,' said God. 'Now we have sea and land.'

God covered the dry land with plants. Little green shoots grew to tall golden grain for the harvest.

There were trees with pink and white
blossom.

'That's good,' said God. 'There will
soon be ripe fruit to eat and nuts to
enjoy.'

There were shiny leaves of vines
climbing around the trees. God could
smell the scent of the flowers he had
made.

'What a beautiful earth it will be,'
he said.

10

He felt the rough bark on the huge oak trees. He saw the ferns uncurling their leaves from the damp earth.

'That's good,' said God.

God knew the plants needed warm light. He made the sun to shine in the daytime.

'That will keep my plants strong and green,' he said.

God knew he was going to make some
animals who would be awake at night.
They would need a light too, but not
such a bright, hot one as the sun.

So God made the moon and stars.

'That's good,' said God.

13

God watched the waves of the sea splashing on the sand. He saw the sun shining on the water. The air smelled of plants and flowers.

'These are good places t⸺
'I will make fish to e⸺
I will make birds v⸺
fly in the air.
    'That's good,' ⸺
have fish in the ⸺
air.'

'Now I shall make some tiny creatures,
like this ant and this buzzing bee,' said
God.

'I shall make some huge animals, like
this elephant and that rhinoceros.

'Some animals will move slowly like this sloth. Some will be very fast like that cheetah. There will be animals of every size and shape.

'That's good,' said God.

God made some of the animals with soft fur and some with hard shells.

The monkeys had strong tails to help them climb, and the owls had big eyes to see in the dark.

Every animal in the sea, the air and on land was perfect.

God looked at them all and smiled. 'That's good,' said God.

Now the earth was ready for people to enjoy.

'I will make people to live here,' said God. So he made a man and a woman.

'That's good,' said God.

'They will have children,' God said.
'Then there will be plenty of people to
take care of my new land.'

God called the man Adam and the
woman Eve. They were his special
friends.

God showed the man and the woman
all the things he had made for them to
enjoy.

'Thank you,' they said. 'This earth is
a beautiful place.'

God looked at the earth. 'Yes, it is a beautiful place,' he said. 'It is very good. Now I can rest and enjoy it.'

So God rested after all his work, and enjoyed everything he had made.

**The Lion Story Bible** is made up of 52 individual stories for young readers, building up an understanding of the Bible as one story – God's story – a story for all time and all people.

The Old Testament section (numbers 1-30) tells the story of a great nation – God's chosen people, the Israelites – and God's love and care for them through good times and bad. The stories are about people who knew and trusted God. From this nation came one special person, Jesus Christ, sent by God to save all people everywhere.

*In the beginning* comes from the very first chapter of the Bible, the Old Testament book of Genesis, chapter 1. It tells us that our world did not simply begin by accident. It was planned and created by God. He made everything there is, and he made it good. When all was ready he made man and woman to take charge of the world and care for every creature. Above all, mankind was made to have a special relationship to God, to communicate freely with him as his friends.

How this relationship was spoiled is told in the next story in this series, number 2: *Adam and Eve*.